Southwest Indians Coloring Book

PETER F. COPELAND

DOVER PUBLICATIONS, INC.
NEW YORK

To Carmen Elise Alston

Introduction

The country of the Southwest Indians—New Mexico, Arizona, southwest Nevada, southern Colorado, southern Utah and the California border—is quite different from the flat plains of central Texas and Oklahoma to the east, and the deserts and coastal ranges of California to the west. It is a wild, awe-inspiring, often inhospitable country.

A land of little rainfall and few rivers, a rugged country of dusty flat-topped mesas, steep-walled canyons and yellow-pine forests, it is strung with mountain ranges. The summers are burning hot and the winters fierce with gales and driving snow.

The southwest Indian people speak languages from five different linguistic families. They are mainly farmers and herders, working a dry country, raising crops of corn, beans, squash, tobacco and cotton, as well as sheep and cattle. They are skilled weavers, potters and basketmakers whose products are world-famous. They have developed a sophisticated system of irrigation, vital in their arid homeland.

In some areas the people still live much as their ancestors did centuries ago, especially in the Pueblo villages along the Rio Grande river. Religion has played, and continues to play, a large part in their traditional way of life.

Bibliographical Note

Southwest Indians Coloring Book is a new work, first published by Dover Publications, Inc., in 1994.

DOVER *Pictorial Archive* SERIES

This book belongs to the Dover Pictorial Archive Series. You may use the designs and illustrations for graphics and crafts applications, free and without special permission, provided that you include no more than four in the same publication or project. (For permission for additional use, please write to Dover Publications, Inc., 180 Varick Street, New York, N.Y. 10014).

However, republication or reproduction of any illustration by any other graphic service whether it be in a book or in any other design resource is strictly prohibited.

International Standard Book Number: 0-486-27964-2

Manufactured in the United States of America
Dover Publications, Inc., 31 East 2nd Street, Mineola, N.Y. 11501

White Mountain Apache women, 1950. These Apache women are climbing the White Mountain, sacred to their people, who call it "Dzil Digai," home of the wind and the mountain spirits. The tribal reservation of the White Mountain Apache people lies within their old ancestral homeland. The tribal council has turned this natural resource to a profit with logging, fishing lakes and a ski resort.

Traditional Apache cradleboards. Apache babies are still held in traditional cradleboards. Some modern Apache women consider the cradleboard a safe car seat. Cradleboards are made at home, using desert plants, sotol for the boards, and cholla cactus for the canopy. A skilled Apache woman can assemble 20 of these cradleboards in a year.

A Zuni man of wealth. The Zuni people are pueblo dwellers, living on an arm of the Little Colorado river in New Mexico. The massive turquoise necklace worn by this Zuni marks him as a man of wealth. The captive eagle at his side is kept for its feathers, which are plucked for use in religious ceremonies.

A Pima basketmaker. For five centuries the Pima people have been famed in the Southwest as basketmakers. This Pima woman has stripes tattooed on her chin, an antique and highly esteemed feminine decoration. Her husband wears his hair longer than the women do and ties it at the end into a clublike knot. The Pima, unlike many of the Pueblo people, live in one-family houses like the dome-shaped one seen at the right. Thatched roof and walls are supported by stout posts. The Pima people live along the Gila river in south-central Arizona.

Navaho medicine men, 1988. Ceremonial dress has always played an important part in the lives of Southwest Indians and it does so to this day. The man on the left wears the ancient traditional dress and the man on the right wears a modern adaptation of the ceremonial tribal costume.

A Mescalero Apache chief and woman. In days gone by, the Apache were a warlike people who frequently conducted cattle raids upon their neighbors. The Apache boy was trained to be an expert warrior and, though girls were brought up to be wives and mothers, they were known often to accompany their men in raiding parties.

A Pueblo woman carrying her baby, 1890. This woman carries her baby wrapped in a blanket. She walks before the ruin of the ancient pueblo of Pecos in New Mexico.

Pueblo man playing a wooden flute, 1890. His flute is unchanged from the type used for many centuries by the Indians of the Southwest. Historically, the flute was used in the ritual of courtship and in healing ceremonies. Among the Zuni people flutes are made not of wood but of ceramic clay.

A modern Hopi farmer in the scorching desert sun.
The little patches of corn in his small garden look
parched and stunted in the hot sun. The Hopi people
grow several varieties of corn upon their arid land without extensive irrigation. Legend tells us that they sing,
talk and pray to the corn so that it may survive the dry,
burning climate.

Hopi women weaving baskets. These Hopi women collect the materials for basketmaking in the gathering season, then dry, preserve and prepare those parts of the plants which they intend to use. Their tools are few: fingers, teeth, a knife and shells or stones for polishing. The inset basket is an ornately decorated one woven by the Pomo people of southern California. Basketry is the most ancient of Native American crafts.

Modern Hopi Kachina dancers. At the 16-day-long Hopi bean festival, weirdly masked, garishly painted dancers distribute fruit and other gifts as reminders of divine beneficence.

Two Apache chiefs of 1886. These two Apache warriors are in the style of dress worn by the last hostile Apaches who fought the whites under Geronimo in 1886.

Navajo fire dance, 1845. At the end of the Mexican War in 1848, the land of the Navajos (northern New Mexico and Arizona) became part of the United States. In a series of wars between the whites and the Navajo people the Navajos were successful in keeping the encroaching white settlers away from their land. Under the leadership of the frontiersman Kit Carson, U.S. armed forces destroyed the herds and flocks of Navajo sheep,

cattle and ponies, cut down their orchards and destroyed their small farms. Eventually more than 8,000 Navajos surrendered to U.S. forces and were moved to a reservation far to the east of their homeland at Bosque Redondo near the Texas border. Here we see Navajo warriors engaged in a traditional fire dance in the mid-nineteenth century.

Three generations of a modern Navajo family.
These three female members of a modern Navajo family,
in traditional dress, replete with silver and turquoise
squash-blossom necklaces, gather at the door of their
dwelling, a traditional Navajo hogan.

Navajo braves of a vanished time. Here we see two Navajo braves as they looked before falling under the influence of the Pueblo people. The Navajos are closely related to the Apaches, and these braves resemble Apache hunters on the trail.

Navajo mother and children, 1900. The Navajos were much influenced by the Pueblo people, from whom they learned weaving and farming. They began wearing Pueblo-style woolen blankets and cotton clothing in the late 1800s. Women wore velveteen shirts and long skirts like those popular in Europe. Here we see a Navajo mother and her children. Her baby is secure in an Apache-style cradleboard.

Zuni turquoise driller. Both the Navajo and the Zuni people are famed for their silverwork. There is a difference between the work of the two peoples, however. The Navajo silversmith uses silver more exclusively in his designs whereas the Zuni incorporates more turquoise in his creations. Here we see a Zuni turquoise driller with his simple hand drill and bench. Around him may be seen some examples of Navajo and Zuni silversmithing: conchas, beads, necklaces, and buckles of silver and turquoise.

Navajo man and woman of 1890. The costume of the Navajo people of the last century was quite colorful. The man's shirt was usually brilliantly colored, green, purple, crimson or blue, and confined at the waist with a belt of silver conchas. His serape was also brilliantly colored and his trousers were often of striped or varicolored cloth. The woman's skirt was made of cotton and very full. She wore a number of silver conchas and other silver decorations on her dress. Her hair was clubbed at the back and wrapped in white woolen string.

A Navajo weaver. Until 1900 most Navajo weaving was used for clothing and equipping the tribe, but traders soon saw a market for Navajo weaving and today the closely woven Navajo rug is sold all over the world as a proud symbol of the talent and industry of the Navajo.

Hopi potters. Manufacturing methods among the Pueblo potters have changed little in the centuries since the Spanish conquistadores discovered them. Those shown here have inherited the skills of the ancient Pueblo dwellers. The painter in the foreground applies a free-hand design to a pot with a brush made of fringed yucca leaf. The pot is fired in a wood fire for about an hour, after which the fire is dampened to smolder. The pot is left there for another half-hour before being allowed to cool.

Mohave man and woman of the 1870s. The Mohaves of southern California were a farming people in the nineteenth century. The women planted crops in the narrow fields along the banks of the Colorado river while the men engaged in frequent warfare and raiding parties. Facial tattooing was practiced among the Mohave people at that time.

Yuma braves of 1862. Here we see two members of the Yuma tribe in southern California. The Mohaves and the Yuma are closely related and both were warlike. These men wear garments of rabbit skin.

White Mountain Apache warriors of 1875. The last hostile Apache warriors in the old southwest did not surrender until Geronimo and his band of so-called "ren- egades" gave up the struggle in 1886. Here we see some White Mountain Apache warriors in 1875.

Tusayan field shelter. When traveling far from home, the Pueblo people erected temporary shelters like the one seen here as dwellings for the night. Constructed simply of brush and branches, such a shelter offered adequate protection from wind and weather.

A room in a Zuni pueblo house. The Zuni pueblo house was a multistoried building with thick walls that kept the people cool in the summer and warm in winter. Entrance to the dwelling was by means of a ladder, which could, for safety, be removed in time of war. Here we see women grinding corn grown, with great effort, upon the parched desert land.

A scene in Hano, 1880. The pueblo villages of Walpi, Sechumovi (or Sichomovi) and Hano are built atop a mesa or butte (a mountain with a flat top) rising 300 to 400 feet above the plain. The pueblo dwellings were built of brick made from sun-dried adobe.

Navajo woman weaving a belt. Among the Pueblo people it is the men who weave; among the Navajos, however, women are in charge of the weaving industry and practice of the art. The designs that Navajo women weave are passed down from mother to daughter. Here we see a Navajo woman weaving a belt upon a primitive narrow loom.

Hopi priest and woman dressed for the snake dance, 1885. At the beginning of the snake dance, Hopi medicine men gathered rattlesnakes into a great writhing, rattling, hissing mass. The priests used a feathered wand like the one carried by this man to gather the snakes into a pile. Each snake was seized by a priest, who held it between his teeth and danced while the snake writhed around his hands and arms. After the dance the snakes were given their freedom. Hopi girls wear their hair in whorls resembling squash blossoms, which symbolize fertility.

Modern Yuma woman and baby.
The houses of the Yuma people are flat-roofed structures built of poles and walled with cactus rods or brush and sometimes plastered with adobe. The front often has a deep, sheltered, shaded area somewhat like a porch, a cool place for daily life in the hot California border country. This Yuma mother is dressed in conventional Anglo-American clothing.

Indian Service range manager instructing Hopi men in sheep care. Most Hopi families own sheep or cattle. The men of the tribe spend much of their time raising sheep and must spend long periods of time away from home at sheep camps.

Hopi students at Oraibi High School, 1940. Students attending Indian Service schools are exposed to the wide world outside their pueblo. They meet children of other pueblos, their horizons widen and their loyalty to their pueblo (some say) is shaken. Indian boys learn such trades as blacksmithing, auto mechanics and carpentry in the school shops, and many, after graduation, leave their pueblo to seek jobs in such places as Albuquerque or Gallop, or on the Santa Fe railroad.

Papago woman cooking tamales. This Papago wife is putting tamales into a steaming pot. The structure in the background is an earthen oven that is used to bake bread when many people are to be fed. Cooking is done outdoors in good weather.

Old man and woman of Taos, 1899. This elderly couple of the Taos Pueblo in New Mexico are the descendants of the ancient Pueblo Indians, whose traditions in the land go back over 2000 years, before the white man came, when the land was theirs.

The Tcirkwena, or skipping dance of the Papago people. The Papago, or "bean people," live in southern Arizona. One of their reservations is at San Xavier del Bac near Tucson. These Papagos are seen at Sells, Arizona, where they hold ceremonial dances and have a rodeo each October.

Acoma woman baking bread. This woman of the Acoma pueblo in New Mexico is baking bread in a beehive-like oven, in which the hottest fire possible is kindled, then scraped out of the oven. The bread is then placed on the hot oven floor to bake. A slab of rock is placed over the door, its edges sealed with mud so that no vapors can escape while the bread is baking.

A potter firing pottery at Hano, 1901. American Indian pottery is made entirely without the use of the potter's wheel. The pot is shaped by hand and smoothed with special smoothing stones. The pot is thoroughly dried before baking in fire as seen here.

Mescalero Apache cowboy, 1940. Cattle raising became an important activity of the Mescalero Apache people in the early twentieth century. In 1934 a cattle growers' association was established on the Mescalero reservation to manage the business of stock raising. The cattle industry has been one of the most profitable enterprises at Apache reservations in New Mexico and Arizona.

Apache woman building a wickiup. The wickiup, the Apache dwelling, has historically been built by squaws from materials readily at hand. Wooden poles are set a few inches into the ground, the tops are fastened together and a covering of grass or brush is laid on, often covered over with bits and pieces of canvas or old clothing. The structure can be built in a few hours. Small wickiups are built for short stays, whereas winter quarters, as seen in the background here, are larger and more sturdily built. In good weather, cooking is done outdoors and in winter it is done inside, the smoke from the fire escaping through a hole at the top.

Tribal drum makers, 1970. These men of Taos Pueblo are making drums. The man at the left is beginning to core a log that will be the shell of a small drum. The man at the right is testing the cords and the tone of a new drum. At the bottom we see a drum with a wooden body, cowhide heads and lashing, and a beater.

A young Navajo shepherd, 1979. This young Navajo shepherd with a part of his flock is seen in front of the 4 Corners Power Plant at Fruitland, New Mexico. The picture might represent the coexistence of traditional and modern sources of livelihood for the native American peoples of the Southwest.